Haunted Poems
And
Hunted Shadows

S. E. McKenzie

S. E. MCKENZIE

ISBN: **1928069207**

ISBN-13:
978-1-928069-20-1

"Somewhere beyond right or wrong there is a garden and I will meet you there" Rumi

S. E. MCKENZIE

TABLE OF
CONTENTS

I AM THE POEM

I am the poem,
I am the instrument for creation,
I can create any sensation.

I am the poem,
Fire when I feel cold,
Youth when I feel old.

I am the poem,
Makes me high,
Makes me cry.

I am the poem,
A Universal love,
That comes from my heart.

I am the poem,
That may keep us together,
When other words may tear us apart.

S. E. MCKENZIE

WHY I LOVE YOU

Oh, you came to me,
When I was all alone,
In a world as cold as stone,
That is why I love you.

You picked me up
When I was down,
You kissed away my frown,
That is why I love you.

You gave me a reason to dream,
While the world made me wanna scream,
You took my hand; I was under your command,
That is why I love you.

And if you should go away,
I will love you anyway,
You brought new meaning to my life
That is why I love you.

MELTED ICE

We built the walls,
To hide away.
We built the walls,
So we would have a place to stay.

Feel the ice melt
In all this heat.
Feel the ice melt
At your feet.

Do not become blinded by the tears.
You need clear eyes to see through the fears.
The reaction to all the years
When you had no walls.

S. E. MCKENZIE

THE LITTLE GREEN THING

Hope for hope's sake,
To the tune of the Skin Drum,
Hoping for peace of mind,
While searching for the Little Green Thing

Lost during Rush Hour.
I wonder who knows
Where the Little Green Thing is.
It may have been blown away by all this rush,
Still I hope to draw upon its Holy Energy,

For the Little Green Thing has
Written "In God we Trust" All over it.
Within its hyper-active soul
The two faced God Head haunts you

While the Little Green Thing, Is still lost.
Now, you must really hope before you see,
The Little Green Thing alive,

It beats to the tune of the Skin Drum,
To the beat so slow but hard.
The little Green Thing is floating away
It is never able to stay.

MISS EAGLE

Hey Miss Eagle
What can you see?
Have you found
Your destiny?

Your eggs are crushed
You are marked with ink
In twenty five years
You could become extinct

You are the queen of the sky
Why I watch you I get high
You are the symbol of the nation
Why do you live in starvation?

S. E. MCKENZIE

TO A DEAD GUITAR

I was falling,
And you broke my fall,
But I crushed you,
And now I feel so small.

What will I do
Without you?
You always helped me sing my song,
You would always play along.

And now you are broken,
Maybe beyond repair.
Today, I awoke, and you weren't there.
I wrote this song cause I'll always care.

Oh gorgeous piece of wood.
Strings so harmoniously inclined,
You brought out the music from within my mind.
Oh what will I do without you?

I was falling
And you broke my fall
But I crushed you
And now I feel so small.

DEAD MAN

He broke his back
To earn his daily bread
They said his pain
Was just in his head

Now all he does is wait
For the change of the state
When a dead man
Comes from the sky

She made a home
Out of her love
When the promise was broken
The pain had awoken

Now all she does is wait
For the change of the state
When a dead man
Comes from the sky.

So frozen in time
It made them shiver
While the vampire
Sucked them dry.

S. E. MCKENZIE

GOLDEN WINGS

I was looking for my higher power,
I was looking for it all day,
The sun could not shine,
The clouds were in the way.

You were the one with the golden wings,
You flew into my life.
Like a shadow, you took away my breath,
As you led me out of this valley of death.

Then you covered me with your Golden wings,
You looked into my soul of fire,
You made me blind with desire,
And all I could do was close my eyes.

When I awoke in the middle of the night,
All I wanted to do was hold you tight,
But you left me all alone,
So I could grow wings of my own.

ATOMIC ACHE

I don't want atomic Ache
Cause I wanna do it again
Again and again.

Love generates electricity,
In the maze of Relativity,
Please spare me your hate.

Hate is a communicable disease.
And Hate is so hard to please.
In the maze of relativity.
Please spare me your hate.

I wanna hear your heart music so fine,
I wanna hear it real close to mine.
I know love generates electricity,
In the maze of relativity.

So don't get me con-fused.
Cause I don't want to be misused,
Cause I wanna do it again,
Again and again

S. E. MCKENZIE

MOTION

There is motion in Creation.
Like magic energy grows without explanation.
Was Motion meant to be lived?
As cycles can never be rushed,
You learn to be patient
And the creation will create itself.

There is motion in co-motion
That is felt quicker than words can explain?
Why is love so seldom thanked?
Is your love's strength being weakened by illusion?

So, let your soul flower bloom and feel that light,
Take the time, take all night.
As motion moves all around, floating in air,
Sometimes invisible, sometimes in full bloom,
I try to take it all in.

THE METALLIC TYRANNY

Do you see the thing?
They fight for the thing.
They work for the thing.
They pray to the thing.

The thing can make them sing,
Praise unto the thing.
While the thing
Rules their minds.

They count their gold
While they get old
Then the thing rusts
And fades away.

MENTAL RANGE

Mental Range:
Root system,
Branching out,
From the seedy origin,
Of Relative desire,
Captivated by the impact of the moment.

External Mental Range:
Rising and Falling,
Sometimes visibility is reduced,
By tear drops blurring the eyes,
When same old promise has been broken again.
Could you appreciate pleasure,
If you never felt pain?

Internal Mental Range:
Creative and destructive,
Capacity to value self,
"Peace" a state of mind?
A quality of consciousness,
Not yet disturbed by the outside mental range

THE IMAGE AND THE SHADOW

See your shadow?
It shall follow
Only You and who walks beside you.

And for the rest of your life,
People shall see,
Only what they want to see.

Sometimes I wonder if
To be blinded by the skin
Was the original sin.

I see the human spirit
So deep inside you
I see the Hidden force inside me too.

Can you feel the force so alive?
We need this force to survive.
And as we watch it grow

From yesterday, until tomorrow
The life force seems to also know
When it's time to go.

S. E. MCKENZIE

CURRENTS

If I tried to reach the sky today,
What would get in the way?
If I try to live without my dream,
Could I really cross this forbidden stream?

Currents wave so strongly,
And I am on the edge,
Of tomorrow,
When this day goes by.

And the sun will rise again,
So let it shine on me,
While I stay in this zone,
So protected, for I am alone.

I shall hide under this stone,
Do not let it roll,
I am not lost but only broken,
Yesterday, they stole my soul.

BROKEN HEARTED

The broken hearted,
Had lost the feeling,
So they departed,

From the life they had before.
Now they file two by two,
Like the broken hearted often do.

Lost in lost dreams,
Lost in midnight screams,
Lost in a pile of files,

As their children watch.

S. E. MCKENZIE

DO YOU SNEEZE IN THE BREEZE?

Do you sneeze in the breeze?
Do you feel old in the cold?
We all need someone to feed,
Dying in all this greed.

Sometimes I wonder why,
They don't come out and say,
Let's stop the overkill,
Of the underfed today.

And how can we see,
With objectivity,
When so many things are meant to block our sight,
During these dark days with so little light.

What is a revolution without love?
Is it dogma from above?
Will it make us bleed?
Or will we take up ploughs to sew seed?

What gave you the right,
To take over everything in sight?
What gave you the right,
To take over the silence of the night?

LOVE AND I

It was another day,
The sky was grey,
The clouds were in the way,
Of the sun's shine.

I know what is mine,
Love and I,
We try to believe,
So we give it another try.

Makes it all worthwhile,
To see you smile,
Love and I,
Hope it is not a lie.

S. E. MCKENZIE

PRETTY CITY

There was once
A pretty city
Where everyone wanted to go

It was in a green valley
And in the mountains above
There was snow

The pretty city
Soon became a possession
That few would let go.

There were people
That took
Whatever they could

They could kill with a smile
And we knew
That they would

Soon the pretty city
Was divided in two
One side was rich

Pretty City (continued)

The other was blue
And then came a chain
That locked them in pain

And the pain
Destroyed positivity
Love and creativity

And the pretty city
Began to crumble
While the takers could only grumble

But the chain
Was never taken down
So all the producers

Could only leave town
As they left the pain behind
They left a tear drop too

A broken system
Lost in pain
Adorned with a black chain

S. E. MCKENZIE

A CIRCLE

Was he trapped in a circle?
Or was the trap a sphere?
Whatever it was,
It was bounded by fear.

Some said chaos ruled,
Opposing forces,
Contracting, expanding,
Making the sphere spin.

No one knew how the sphere began,
A time before this conception,
Pre-programmed reception,
The collective was waiting.

As tilted poles
Were being pulled
And pushed
By a force unknown

Pressure was building,
While many were trapped inside,
This sphere of fear,
Some called a circle.

THE LINK

He asked love,
How long was forever,
And if she was
Ready to expand.

He asked love to make him stronger,
So that he could understand,
The worlds inside the Earth,
That he will never see.

He is so afraid to live,
But more afraid to die,
He asked love,
If she was just another lie.

S. E. MCKENZIE

LOST IN THE SKY

You were so proud
Held your head high
Never felt lost before
Never been thrown on the floor

Big man of the universe
It was easy to love in your omniverse
Polarized as opposites fight
Believing each one to be right

You aged with time
Forgot how to rhyme
You crumpled your paper in hand
You forgot how to take time to understand

You were not the same
And it showed
No longer big man of the universe
You complained about pain every day

Cause the pain never went away
Until you shot your head off into the wall
And faded into the sky like stardust so small
Bones buried in the ground never make a sound

For they sleep in soft satin

LEARNING

His momma held his hand
Until the task was done
Then he realized that writing
And reading could be fun

Sure he could run
And Jump sort of high,
But when he learned to read and write,
He could fly into the sky and do it all night.

He could be anything he wanted to be
Short tall, young and old.
All those doors were open to him
He could be part of the story,

And he could feel all the glory,
Cause he could do it all.
With knowledge came power,
So he never felt small.

Learning (continued)

Content inside which could only grow
Because it doesn't ever overflow
It connects to the next
And doesn't let go

Thoughts and dreams
That he could believe in.
When all was said
'I think therefore I am'

And he was then able to inspire
As reading and thinking caught fire
It was more than just a dream
It was an ideal to believe in.

His pen became the sword
That never took life.
His pen became the sword
That sought peace during strife.

BEHIND A WALL

Well he couldn't adjust
And his life was a bust
He couldn't find love

And no one could see
The sad man
Lost in the crowd

No one knew his name
Though he had everything a person could desire
But love, everything else, was not enough

He looked for a smile
And he saw no expression at all
They could not see him

For he was living behind a wall

S. E. MCKENZIE

SUSTAIN

You are the man around town
You feel the hype
Believe the stereotype

Hide your gun
Looking for fun
You have a feel like steel

Opposite poles attract
Most of the time anyway
For you, no one will look your way

You are seen with disdain
You feel so much pain
As your magnet turns on you

It is pulled by the steel you feel
And forever it will seem
Like your worst nightmare

That you could ever dream

URBAN SPRAWL

He was so slick
With coat and tie
He was in his expensive car
And he always drove by

He was like a fly
Around honey
While the bees
Were dying all around

But no one would say
That they knew why
As they watched mother nature fume
In the land where many felt doom

REFLECTIONS OF THE DOOMED

He sees his reflection
In your eyes
He can't look away

Soon he says
I freely choose
To despise your eyes

And he went on in life
Feeding his bias in everyway
He saw your eyes

Then looked the other way.
He never had to see
What was in the way?

For the beam in his eye
Made him blind and unkind
Still he was a fool to never question the lie.

Out of context
No process to see
We were doomed under his authority

Some said for eternity.

DECISION

I needed your vision,
Couldn't make a decision,
Had to face the shock,
Block out, become a rock.

I looked into your eyes so blue,
I really didn't know what I should do,
The pain had numbed my brain,
And I was afraid to love again.

You fed me peace and helped me grow,
As you gave me time to recover from my sorrow.
You helped me through the hardest of times
And I thought you would always be there.

Until you died too.

S. E. MCKENZIE

WALKING IN THE RAIN

You liked to watch
So you joined the group
You sat by the window
While eating soup

As the years flew by
You saw many people walk by
Some were black and some were white
Some were blue just like you

Then one rainy night
A man walked into your sight
As you watched him go by
He seemed so happy, it made you cry

You had the gun
He started to run
And then died in his blood
What you called mud.

MY DREAMS

My dreams have rights too,
For they are living blue prints for action,
So that I may live a life
Of Freedom and Satisfaction.

My dreams grow in my head,
The difference between,
Being asleep and being dead.

I awake from my dreams to face the day,
But I don't want my dreams to fade away,
For my dreams are like a candle in the night,

When the world's darkness can bring
So much fear and fright,
That is when I need my dreams to dream at night.

And when doubt clouds my brain,
You know I'll just close my eyes,
So that my dreams
Will have a chance to dream again.

S. E. MCKENZIE

THE WARHEAD

I awoke suddenly in the middle of the night,
To the cries of a warhead.
And then I knew,
What it must have been going through.

And the warhead said:
"I was made from light,
Showed them a bit of might,
Now, I can't sleep at night.

I can't say what is right or wrong,
I was only made to make them strong.
I don't wanna be a tool for a fool,
Don't wanna be made to be so cruel.

I know I create so much fright
As I fly through the sky,
At the speed of light,
I don't know how killing can ever be right.

I know the people who made me
Will never be free,
For they will always be,
Haunted by the karma of me."

And the warhead cried, cause so many died,
And the warhead said:
"I don't wanna be a warhead
All I wanna do is make love instead."

CROW

I saw you Crow
Sitting on a sign
With nowhere to go

You stood there,
Beak in feathers
Power resting

And suggesting
No thoughts
To lose in the fog

Not as noble as an eagle
But still a bird of prey
And you are surviving

In this urban rush
And decay
I hear your grating call

I hear it every day
Anyway
You appear to be at home here

S. E. MCKENZIE

Crow (continued)

You never seem to know fear
What do you have to lose?
You are just a crow

Able and willing
To fly to a place you have never been
To see what has never been seen

Covered in fog
And morning dew
I can still feel the heart in you

Oh Urban vulture
A beast of little culture
Still you adjust and adapt

Below the heavens up high
You fly
Higher than I

So, carry me away
From here
This valley of fear

You leave without a tear

BIG

You are big
You drive yourself
Like a big rig

You have assumptions
And opinions too
Everyone listens to you

You are big
You say this and you say that
No one asks if it is a fact

You are big
We assume
Our doom

I know
The sorrow
Of this gloom

S. E. MCKENZIE

HATE

I am hate.
Feel me grow,
From a seed,
Into tomorrow.

I am hate.
I feed you,
Cause I need you,
Forever blind.

And If I should burn you out,
In my greed, you know, I won't care.
I am hate,
I don't play fair.

MY WIRE

My wire goes through my wall,
And hangs between some poles.
And down the street,

Somehow,
My wire and yours meet,
Between your land and mine.

And at my command,
My wire takes words from my mind,
And brings them to your eyes,

Just naked words with no disguise.
As I let my wire know
I can feel our love grow.

And as my wire fills your room
So freely with my love
My wire knows it will really, never be enough.

And as the borders close their doors,
For a while, we defy what makes some cry.
For a while we become one in one world.

S. E. MCKENZIE

THE MIND WAR

What is a revolution without love?
Is it dogma from above?
Will it make us bleed or will it feed those in need?
Will it breed familiarity as an excuse for contempt?

Will he want to be exempt?
Don't bang that book on his head,
Don't give him dirty looks which say you want him dead
Don't trap him in a mind war of contempt and fear

Cause we all have better things to do and they are so near.

Don't want your misery
Don't want to repeat your history,
As you whisper behind your closed door
We know we have all been there before

What gave you the right
To dominate everything in sight
What gave you the right
To dominate the silence of the night?

The mind war (continued)

What gave you the right
To hurt your neighbour is such a way
He tries to not hate you so
Even when he has lost the game of sum zero

He walks away
Knowing a better way
Than getting trapped in the mind war
We have all been there before.

They have bars to bind you
They have bars to blind you
They even have bars of love
So don't get blinded by the mind war

We have all been there before
We have been down the floor
We have ran out of the door
Begging you to stop the mind war

That is what love is for

S. E. MCKENZIE

CLOSED DOORS

Closed doors surround you
They keep you out
They make you wanna shout

'Let me in
Let the promise begin
Or was it all a lie

Will I
Be walking through the maze
Of locked doors for all my days
Will I become blinded by the gaze

As the days go by"

GROUP THINK

You kick, you march
You wear a shirt
Thick with starch

You wear your cap
The way they all do
You look in the mirror

It is on the right way
You cannot stray
From this group think

Your friends will betray you
Your friends will kick you down
Your friends will be wearing a frown

S. E. MCKENZIE

Group Think (continued)

You are so afraid to stray from group think
So afraid that your friends will make a big stink
So beware the stare the pain will tear

As they will push you away with force
You say I think therefore I am
They say you think like us or go away

You stumble and fall
So sad and all alone
You wonder if you should stray

From this group think and walk away

MAD WORLD

So much excess
Excess fat
Excess this and excess that

You see that person
Don't you hate their hat
There should be a crime

For wearing that
And so safe are we
Driving in our car

Let us throw our butts out of the window
Let us try to hit that person from afar
Lets get him for wearing that hat we hate

We have the power to seal his fate

S. E. MCKENZIE

NOUVEAU GESTAPO

It could have been love at first sight
Until you tried to flex your might.
You had eyes sometimes blue
And sometimes green,

As your gun made you look so mean.

He was born in a slum.
They called him a bum.
They said he was bad,
But I knew he was sad.

He had been in a cage,
I could feel his rage.
As it grew with age,
The future was forgotten,

Nouveau gestapo (continued)

While he just felt rotten,
He couldn't cope,
He needed dope,
The Gestapo's rope.

You were walking on your beat
He was walking on his street
He saw you, he started to run
You shot him, and then dropped your gun.

The street was red
Soaked with the blood
Gushing from his head
He was at peace,
Now he was dead.

S. E. MCKENZIE

THE D.R.A.F.T

The D.R.A.F.T could tear you apart
Your stomach could fight your heart
Your brain could stop acting smart
As you become their human capital

D is for deadly
R is for response
A is for against
F is for free
T is for types

When I wrote that poem
I was thinking at home
Then just like before
You came knocking at my door

Now you say killing is wrong
Now you say you need a new song
Now you say you need me
But how can we love, when we aren't free?

A.W.O.L.

Can't fight this machine war,
Can't fight it any more.
I must stay here like this with you tonight,
To see your hair shine in the morning light.

I have seen what the machine can do
And it is breaking my heart in two.
I have seen the machine explode in their face,
I have seen their blood splattered all over the place.

I have crawled in the mud,
And I felt so cold,
I swam in the sea of blood,
I felt so old.

And I know
This is where
I must be
Sleeping beside you so peacefully.

I don't wanna fight this machine war
I don't wanna do it anymore.
I have seen some divide just to multiply,

S. E. MCKENZIE

A.W.O.L. (continued)

Others kill without hearing a cry.
Some justify this as they eat the pie,
And some mystify it all
cause they know the lie.

I must stay here
Beside you,
That's all
I really need to do.

Let me hide from this machine war,
Let me feel this peace I have never felt before.
I have missed Role-call.
I am now A.W.O.L.

With only one life to live
I must give all the love
I have to give.
I must stay here,

I must feel no fear.
While I am beside you,
Loving you.
This is what I was born to do.

WHERE DO THE CHILDREN SLEEP?

His journey was long,
Some say it will make him strong,
He has done some things wrong,
Mostly so he could belong.

Lost under an open sky,
Too afraid to shout out why,
All he can do is cry,
As he sees so many die.

All I see,
Is the fire
Above me,
So bright and red.

I can't see the warhead overhead,
But yes I know,
It will always be a tool for a fool,
Cause nothing else could be so cruel.

I hear the warhead roar,
It is too loud to ignore,
As it overkills,
The underfed.

S. E. MCKENZIE

Where do the children sleep? (Continued)

Within its rage so wild,
The warhead can't see God in the child,
All torn up, lying in a pool of blood,
All mixed up in the rain and mud.

Let them sleep,
In their home in the sky,
Where they no longer have to cry,
Cause the angels are now singing a lullaby.

And as I walk upon this Earth,
I wait for mercy and all it's worth,
Almost in paradise many are lost in greed,
Even when they had everything
They could ever need.

Why must we feed this fire
Can't you hear him scream,
Why must we feed this fire?
Why can't we live his dream?

COFFEE CUP CHATTER

It felt so right, brought heat into the night,
Gave me warmth when I was cold,
Gave me a spark, when I was feeling old.

When you hold me. And do what you do,
I know it is between me and you,
You whisper your secrets in my ear,
I tell you there is nothing to fear.

You tell me, you will always be near,
Now Echoes from coffee cup chatter,
Hurt you, make you feel sadder,
They are watching me as I am getting madder,

Keeping the promise will always matter.

S. E. MCKENZIE

FROM THE PLACE ON THE HILL

He talks like a drone
He thinks like a clone
He sits on his make believe throne
So sad that he is still all alone

He sees you and he has to stare
He sees you and he has to glare
He sees you so happy and care free
While his hate lubricates his fate

He has no sense of liberty,
So he has been chosen,
To climb the hill.
He waves the flag

He calls you a fag
He glares before the kill
This is his only thrill
While he looks down at you

From his place on the Hill.

YOU CAN'T KILL HATE

You can't kill hate
Many find that out
When it is too late

Trying to kill hate
Will seal your fate
For hate is just a tool

Try to kill hate
You become
The tool's fool

For hate must be transformed
Into something greater
And more noble

Hate must be transformed into love

S. E. MCKENZIE

WHO IS HE?

Who is he?
Who can you see?
Who do you want him
To really be?

The one who is free,
Dying to reach the sky,
To hear the angels sing,
The eternal lullaby?

Who is he?
When he shares his life with you?
He will become someone new
Someone he never knew.

HOW I FEAR YOUR FEAR

How I fear your fear
I can feel it pulsating
When you are near

You call it beautification
To me it looks like a prison nation
You call it the way you see it

You take ownership of the space
Your fear matters more
Than outcome for another

You forgot about your sister and brother
How I fear all your fear
You made a file about me

You gave me no number
Or nothing that I could see
How could I succeed or feel free

So as woe haunted me
I took a walk in the park
And I felt nature's fury

S. E. MCKENZIE

How I fear your fear (continued)

The wind was strong
The air was flowing
High and low pressure

All mixed up
It made wind around me
And you too

The food chain
Was not right or wrong
And not always green

Red blood flowing
In a holy stream
For life was a gift

Often began
With a scream
I am who I am

How I fear your fear (continued)

And as the waters rose
I hoped for a purpose
From nature almighty

Safe from Earth's fury
Which creates and destroys
As the wind fed

The Earth's fury even more
It freed us
From the prison state of hate

We had one purpose
Which was to survive
We needed to keep

The skin drum alive
Don't wanna be
Fooled by propaganda

S. E. MCKENZIE

How I fear your fear (continued)
Don't wanna be
A missing woman
In Canada

I want to be
Equal to you
Cause that is the only way

That I could ever
Be free enough
To Love you

IN CHARGE

Who put you in charge?
They all said
Oh little girl
That bin lid could have capitated your head.

Who put you in charge?
You just pay the bill
Who put you in charge?
We just kick you down for a thrill.

And then they said

"And if you should be
In the same waiting room as me
I will make such a fuss
I will get them to tell you to take a bus."

And then they said

You just pay the bill
And we kick you down
For our daily thrill.

S. E. MCKENZIE

THE YEARS WENT BY

It was just another day
Lou was just a kid
Going to school
In the usual way.

There was a teacher
Smiling in front of the class
She said if they followed the rules
They were all bound to pass.

Lou tried to sit in his seat
But there was something inside him
Causing him heat
Then he landed up on his feet
And he went to his locker to get something to eat.

There was a policeman in the hall
He told Lou that he could make him crawl"
For breaking the rule
And for being in the hall.

The years went by (continued)

So Lou tried to do
What he was told
Though he could not hold
This thought in his mind.

At the end of the day
Lou went home on the bus.
Lou forgot his homework.
Everyone made a fuss.

The teacher stopped smiling at Lou.
She made him stand in the corner
With a dunce cap on his head.
As they laughed at him until he ran away
And hid in his bed for the rest of the day.

And the years went by
And what could Lou do
He thought he found love
Like everyone wanted to do.

The years went by (continued)

It is sad but true; Lou's wife did not know to do too.
So she said she was going to leave immediately
If Lou didn't go and see
Dr. Joe Inc. who could have the missing link.

Dr. Joe Inc. looked at Lou in the eye,
And asked him what he did to get by.
He prescribed to Lou a pill with great power
It helped him slow down to smell that flower.

The red one that was called a rose,
But in the middle of the day
The pill's power went away
And the chaos inside Lou arose.

And then everyone laughed at Lou
It was true. So Lou screamed out in his pain
"The pill only lets me be like you
For about four hours so what can I do?"

And then the door was slammed
In Lou's face again.

The years went by (continued)

And the years went by
Until the day the man who counted beans
Was counting the white pills too
And once he was done, he called Lou.

The man said something about the cost
And then Lou felt so lost
Since Lou had no clue
And did not know what else he could do.

Lou knew he would lose the love
He used to get from you
And then the pain it just grew
Lou knew he could never be like you

Lou wasn't sure if it was another lie
Or if it was true that angels were in the sky
Who would be singing a lullaby
To welcome him home, the day Lou chose to die.

As Lou crawled through a tunnel of pain
Lou was surrounded by white light
And as Lou started to fly into the sky
A warhead was passing by.

S. E. MCKENZIE

The years went by (continued)

And screamed "Turn around, don't die,"
As Lou looked at the warhead
In all its glory
The warhead took another moment
To tell Lou his story

Then the warhead asked Lou
What he could do
"Why was I made to cause so much fright?
So that war does not seem to be so mean and gory?

And I know my power gives fools
Too much might
I don't want to be like this,
Because it is just not right".

And the warhead said
"If I had my way,
I would be making love every day
And then the warhead
Cried when it remembered
The many who had died.

The years went by (continued)

And the warhead said
Do you think I want?
To hear them scream?
Do you think
I want to ruin their dream?

And even though their dreams
May get broken anyway
I don't want to be the one
To do that to them today.

So could you turn around?
And remember,
Take a minute
To land on the ground

Then could you just speak for me Lou
Could you say this in a crowd?
And could you say it real loud
Maybe Earth is Paradise lost

And maybe if you could turn
All their greed and hate around
You would give your love a chance to shine
And maybe you could save your world in time."

THE END

ANOTHER S. E. McKENZIE PRODUCTION
(A WORK IN PROGRESS)

S. E. MCKENZIE

This book is a book of speculative fiction.
Characters, companies, governments, places, events, are
either products of the author's imagination or used
fictitiously. Any resemblance to persons (living or
dead), companies, governments, places and/or events, is
a coincidence.

Produced by S.E. McKenzie Productions
First Print Edition 2014

Enquiries: 1(778)992-2453
Mailing Address:
S. E. McKenzie Productions
168 B 5th St.
Courtenay, BC
V9N 1J4

Email Address:
messidartha@aol.com

www.ingramcontent.com/pod-product-compliance
Lightning Source LLC
Chambersburg PA
CBHW060535030426
42337CB00021B/4269